Contents

Introducing Crazy Quilting

This circa 1870–1889 crazy quilt was made by Mary Ann (Mann) Rohrer and is in the collection of the Lancaster Mennonite Historical Society, Lancaster, Pennsylvania.

Crazy quilting is a specific kind of patchwork (piecing). Irregularly shaped pieces of fabric are sewn together into a collage of textures and colors.

The style was popular in Colonial times when women sought to make use of every bit of fabric, recycling clothing to patch worn-out coverlets. In Victorian times, the trend became more extravagant. Women sewed bits of fancy fabrics—silk, velvet, and satin—into blocks, and then into coverlets. The seams were decoratively embroidered, and the whole piece was sometimes embellished with beads, lace, ribbon, and buttons.

Getting started

Creating a stocking provides an excellent introduction to crazy quilting. Make one to give as a gift or to keep for yourself. Names and dates can be added to mark milestones such as births, graduations, and weddings.

Your stocking can be individualized by using fabrics in a variety of colors and textures. Your choice of embroidery stitches and floss colors further express your individuality.

We suggest you first make Stocking 1, beginning on page 6. It is a relatively simple stocking with a limited amount of decorative embroidery. Detailed, step-by-step instructions, photographs, and illustrations serve as your guide for its creation. If you choose to begin with one of the other stockings, it is important that you review the instructions for Stocking 1, as the other stockings build on the information and techniques presented there.

The other six stockings can be made following the piecing process described for Stocking 1. Each stocking has numbers indicating the suggested order for piecing, along with a list of materials and other helpful information.

You'll find tips on combining colors, working with textures, patterns for embroidery, and more.

Feel free to follow the examples closely or use them as starting points. Don't hesitate to simplify the designs by using a single patch in place of multiple small patches. Adapt the examples freely, or use them as a stimulus for your own work.

You may decoratively stitch all of these stockings with variations of the featherstitch (directions on page 13). Directions are also included for the French knot, blanket stitch, seed stitch, running stitch, and lazy daisy stitch.

Keep the following in mind when you select fabric:

- There are many fabrics from which to choose. Consider velvet, velveteen silk, wool, cotton, satin, corduroy, linen, rayon velvet, taffeta, brocade, or silk-like polyester.
- Instead of buying all new fabrics, you might want to use remnants from other projects.
- Lay out different fabric combinations to get an idea of what works well together.
- Consider your planned decorative stitching. If your fabric is heavily ornamented or wildly patterned, it will compete with your embroidery.
- A dense or stiff fabric may be difficult to stitch.
- A dark, rich color on the cuff and toe will visually frame the stocking.

Stocking pattern

Enlarge this pattern to 175% for the actual stocking size. The seam allowance is ½" (13mm).

The tools and materials listed here are needed for all of the stockings. See each stocking page for the fabrics and embroidery thread specific to that stocking.

TOOLS

Fabric scissors
Sewing machine
Iron
Fabric pins
Embroidery needle
Tailor's chalk
Rotary cutter and mat (optional)

MATERIALS

Photocopy of pattern
⅓ yd. (⅓m) muslin fabric for base
⅓ yd. (⅓m) fabric for lining
⅓ yd. (⅓m) fabric for back
¼ yd. (¼m) each of a variety of fabrics
Thread to blend with the majority of fabrics
Variety of embroidery floss
Ribbon, cord, or fabric for hanger

TIP: Backing the stocking with the same color fabric as the top cuff and toe on the front pulls the stocking together attractively.

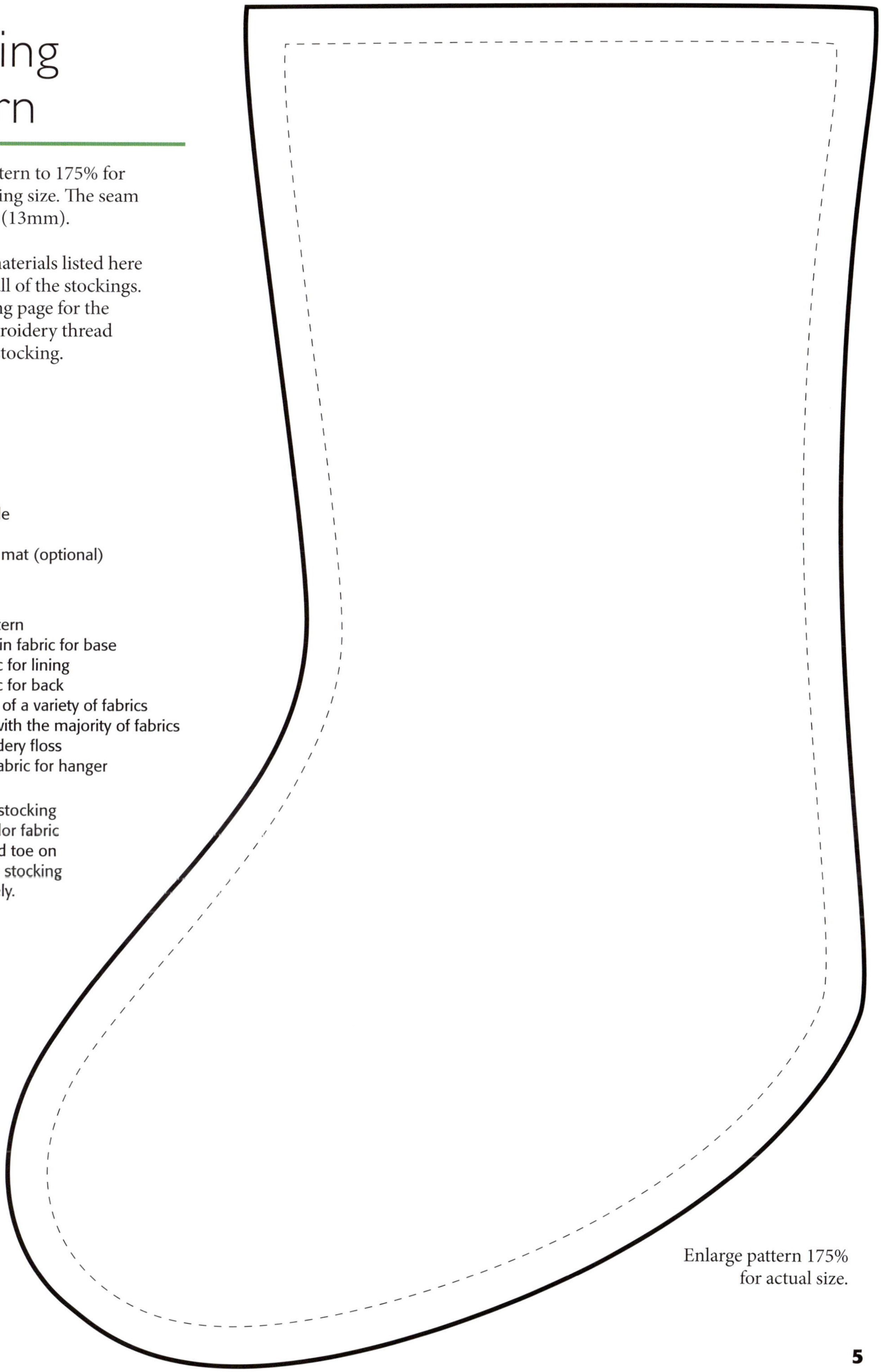

Enlarge pattern 175% for actual size.

5
2
4
1
3
6
7
7
7
7
8
7
9

Stocking 1: Preparation

SPECIFIC TO **STOCKING 1**

Fabrics:

- Black and dark burgundy velvet
- Antique gold silk
- Olive green and burgundy satin
- Olive green crepe
- Blue-green velveteen
- Teal moiré

Embroidery floss:

- Gold, olive green, burgundy, teal, blue-green, and metallic gold

You may want to sketch your design out on a paper copy of the stocking pattern, and then use it as you select fabric and cut the pieces, or you may wish to select fabric from your chosen palette as you go.

When piecing your crazy quilt stocking, you will work out from the center. Add patches to the right and left next, then toward the top, and finally toward the toe.

You will follow the same sequence for each patch except the first.

- Pin the patch facedown in place on the front of the muslin stocking base.
- Sew it to the previous patch and to the base.
- Press each patch from the back side of the base after it has been sewn in place. Carefully monitor the temperature, as these fancy fabrics are very sensitive to excessive heat.
- Trim excess fabric outside the edge of the muslin base.

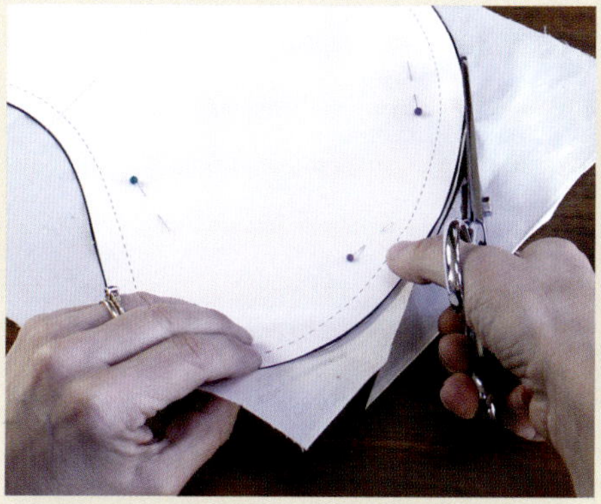

After pinning the pattern to the base muslin, cut out the stocking shape.

Select your fabrics and determine which fabric you want to use for each patch.

Cut fabric pieces roughly to size, allowing 1"–2" (25–51mm) extra fabric all around.

Stocking 1: Piecing

PATCHES 1 AND 2

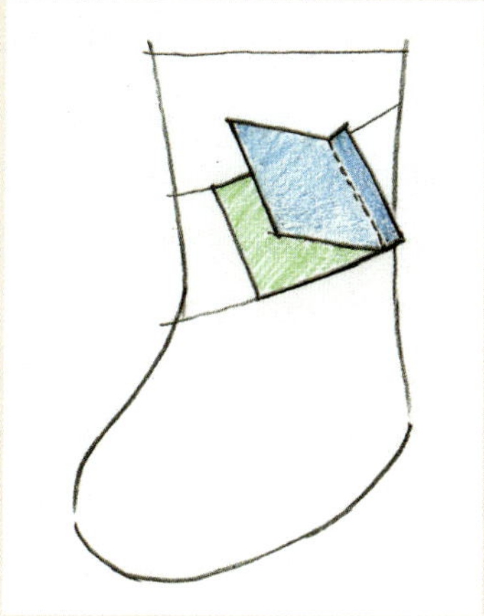

Select the fabric for the center patch (patch 1). Pin it in place right side up.

Pin fabric patch 2 facedown on patch 1 and pin it in place.

Stocking I: Piecing

Sew the common seam, attaching patches 1 and 2 to the muslin base.

Trim excess fabric from patch 2 if needed.

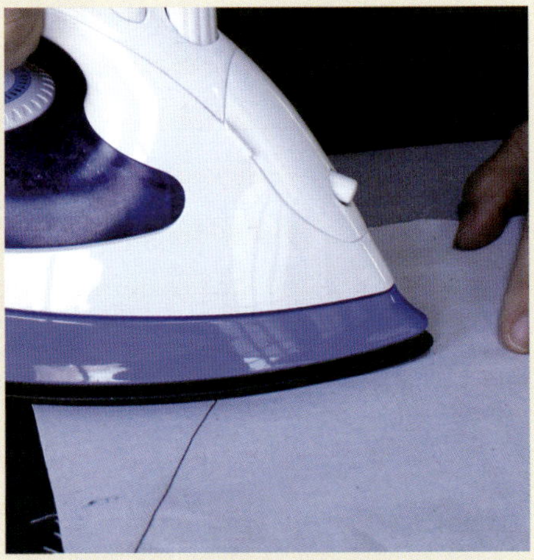

Turn the base with patches 1 and 2 facedown and press.

PATCH 3

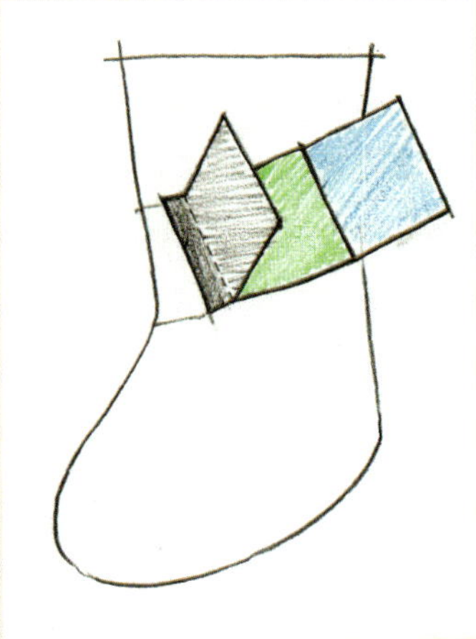

Select patch 3, place it facedown on patch 1, and pin it in place.

Sew the common seam, attaching patch 3 and 1 to the muslin base. Press from the back.

PATCH 4

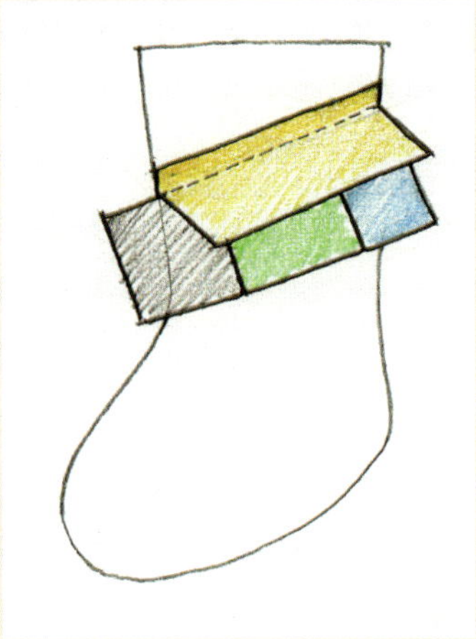

Select patch 4, place it facedown on patches 1, 2, and 3, and pin it in place.

Sew the common seam, attaching patch 4 to the other pieces and to the muslin base. Press from the back.

PATCH 5

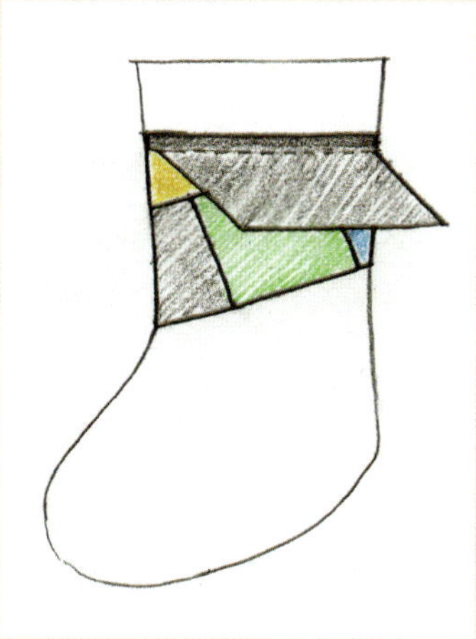

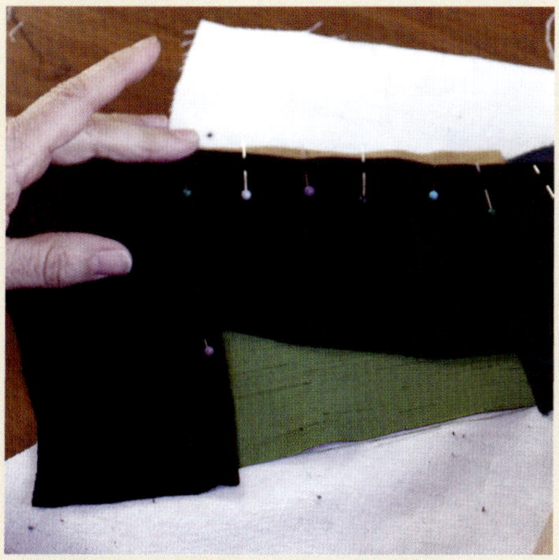

Select and pin patch 5 facedown on patch 4 and sew the common seam. Press from the back.

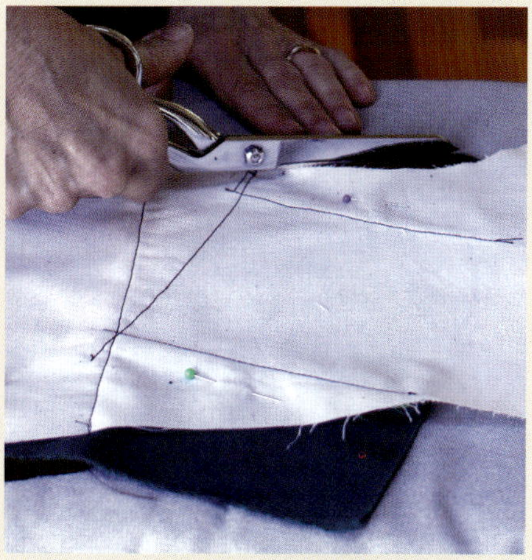

Trim any excess fabric along the outside edge of the muslin base as needed.

PATCH 6

Select patch 6 and place it facedown on patches 1, 2, and 3.

Pin patch 6 in place, sew the common seam, and press from the back.

PATCH 7 (strip)

Select five smaller pieces to form patch 7.

Sew each piece to the next to make a strip.

Stocking I: Piecing

PATCH 7

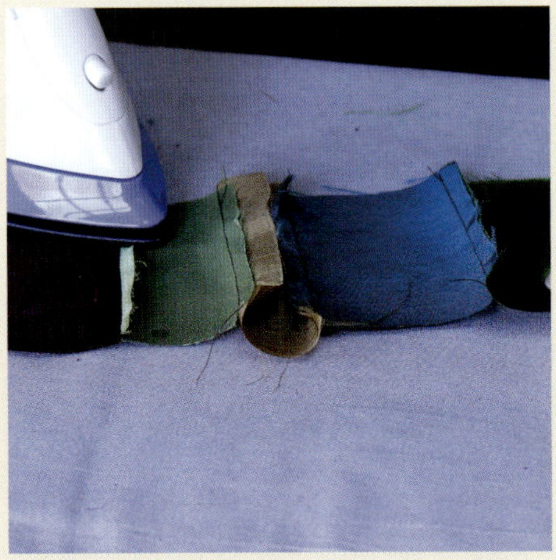

Press the seams open on the five-piece strip that forms patch 7.

Pin patch 7 facedown on patch 6 and the base, and then sew the common seam. Press from the back.

PATCH 8

Select patch 8 and place it facedown on the strip that comprises patch 7.

Pin patch 8 in place, and then sew the common seam. Press from the back.

PATCH 9

Select patch 9, place it facedown on patches 6, 7, and 8, and pin it in place.

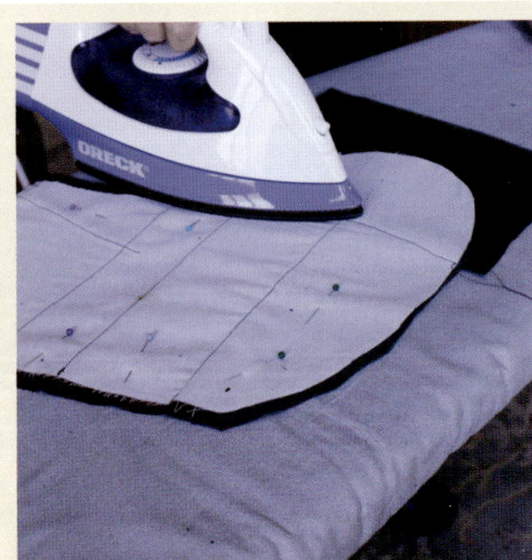

Sew patch 9 in place. Press from the back.

Final attachment of pieces to backing

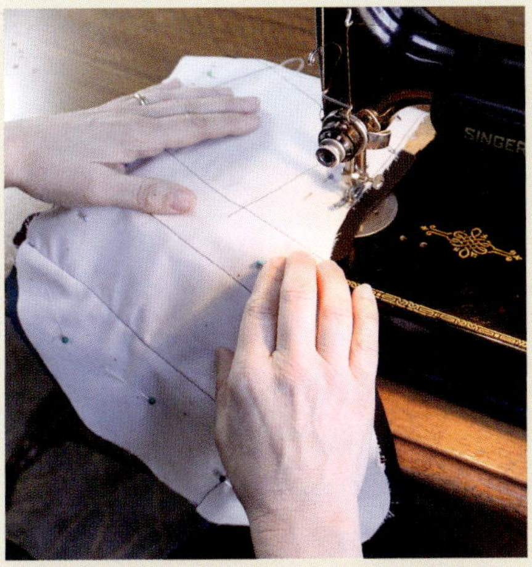
Pin the completed front to the base. Stay stitch ¼" (6mm) in from the edge around the entire muslin piece.

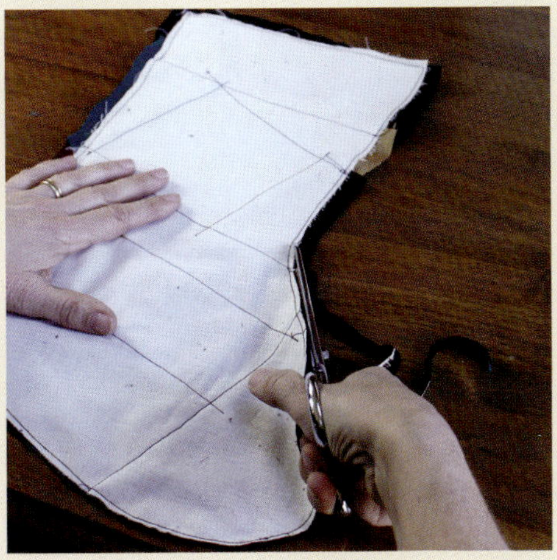
Trim away any fabric that extends beyond the muslin backing.

Now you're ready to embroider!

Stocking 1: Choosing thread

After the stocking is pieced but before the lining and backing are added, it is time to decorate and embellish the stocking with hand embroidery.

Choose embroidery threads in colors and textures that complement and contrast the fabric. You may enjoy a wildly colorful palette or a more subdued effect.

Standard embroidery floss comes in six strands. You may divide the strands and use from one to six, depending on the size of the stitch and the desired look.

You may embroider your stocking with or without an embroidery hoop.

For this stocking, I selected thread in the same color families as the fabrics: gold, olive green, burgundy, teal, and blue-green. I added a metallic gold to bring out the richness and shine of the fabric.

When I placed my stitches, I took care to contrast the thread colors with the fabric colors. I also made sure each thread color was repeated in several parts of the stocking.

Stocking 1: Putting it together

Using the stocking pattern on page 5, cut 2 linings and 1 backing.

1. Pin the hanging loop in place on the outside of the backing just inside of where your seam will be. Sew it securely at the top.

2. Place one lining piece face to face with the embroidered front of the stocking.

3. Align all edges, pin securely, and sew at the top.

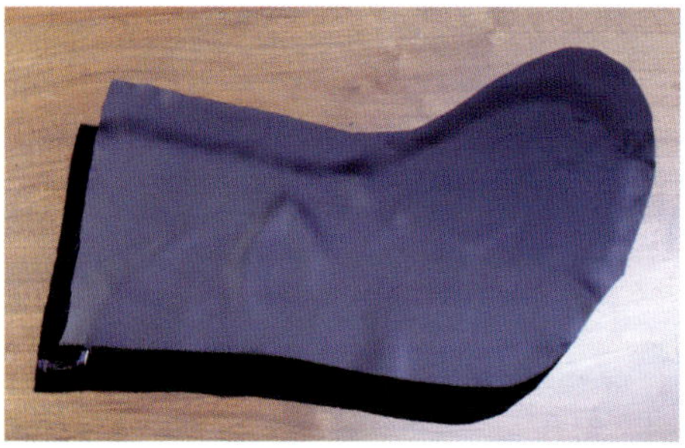

4. Place the second lining piece face to face with the backing, align all edges, pin securely, and sew at the top.

5. Iron the top of each sewn pair, and then stay stitch across the top of the lining to help it lay flat.

6. You now have two long pieces: the back/lining and the front/lining.

7. Place the right sides of the front/lining piece and the back/lining piece together and pin.

8. Sew all around, following just inside the stay stitching. Leave a 3"–5" (76–127mm) opening in the toe end of the lining section so you can turn the stocking right side out.

9. Trim ¼" (6mm) outside of the stitched edge of the embroidered back side of the stocking to remove excess fabric.

10. Turn the stocking right side out.

11. Sew the open toe section of the lining closed.

12. Push the liner inside the stocking. Your stocking is completed!

Embroidery instructions

Featherstitch

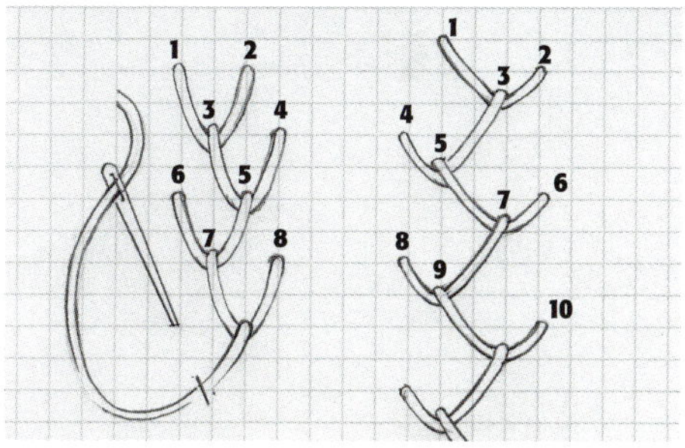

For the featherstitch, bring the needle up at 1, down at 2, and up again at 3, positioning the point of the needle just above the little curve in the thread. Pull the thread all the way through to complete your first stitch. For your second stitch, go down again at 4 and up at 5. Continue in the same fashion, alternating sides.

If your stitches straddle a seam, you'll want to widen the center portion of the stitch to span the seam as the drawing to the right shows.

The featherstitch has many variations. Consider creating a pattern by taking several stitches in one direction, and then one back, as shown in the photograph above. The type and weight of the thread you select will determine the look of the final stitches. The stitches in the top two rows in the photograph above were done with three strands of floss, while the stitches in the bottom row were done with a single strand.

Running stitch

For a basic running stitch (shown above between the two rows of featherstitches), simply weave the needle over and under the fabric. You can take several evenly spaced stitches at a time.

Blanket stitch

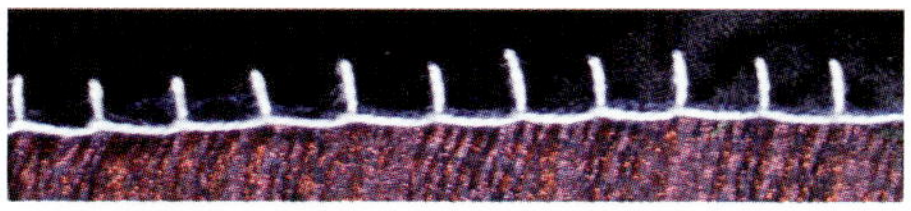

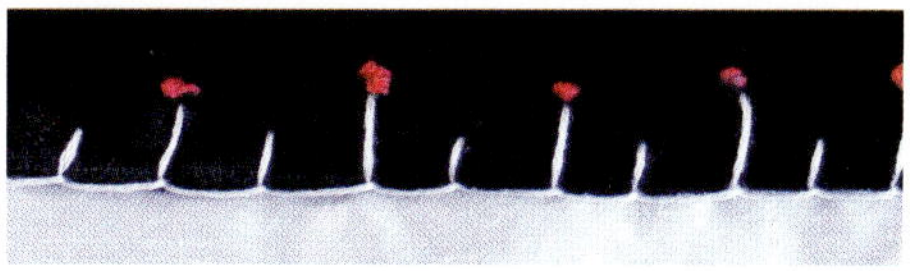

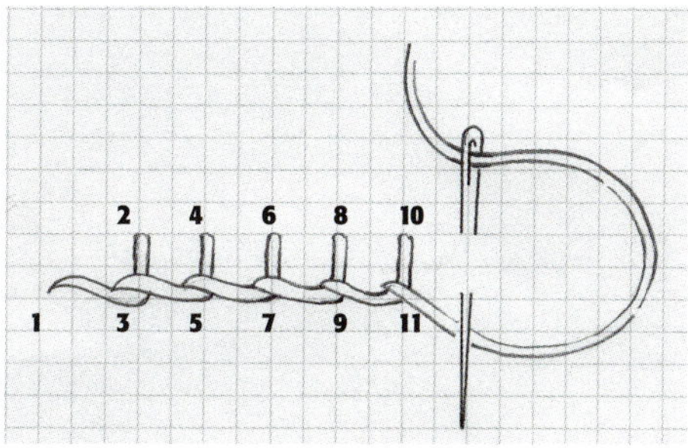

For the blanket stitch, bring the needle up at 1, and then insert it at 2 (diagonally to the right of 1). Take the needle straight down, coming out at 3, looping the thread under the needle point. Go down at 4 and come up at 5. Continue in the same fashion.

You may keep the stitches the same height, or alternate high and low as the photo above shows. Perhaps add French knots for a fun look.

French knot

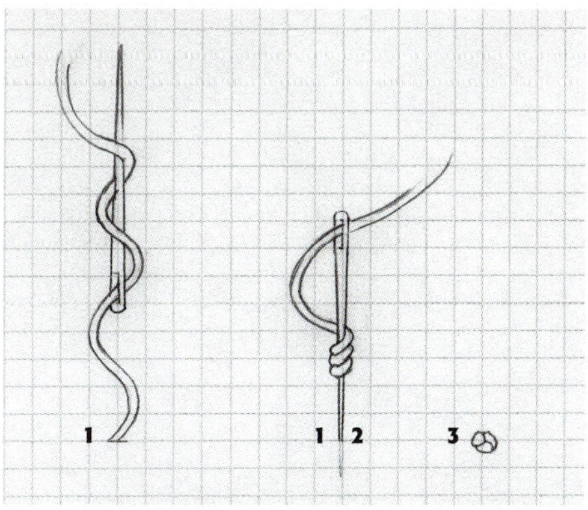

For the French knot, bring the needle up at 1. Wind the thread three times around the needle. Then turn the needle and reinsert it at 2 (very close to 1, but not the same hole). Hold the knot down as you pull the thread through the back (3). Secure it if you want a single knot, or continue to the next if you want multiple knots.

Lazy daisy stitch

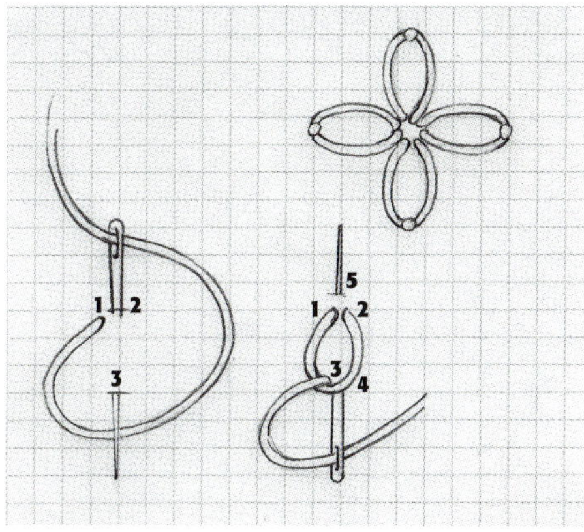

For the lazy daisy stitch, bring the needle up at 1, then reinsert right beside it at 2. Pull the thread to make a small loop and bring the needle up at 3 (inside the loop) and down again at 4 (on the other side of the loop). If making several petals, bring the needle back up at 5 (near holes 1 and 2), and repeat in the desired direction. Daisy petals look sweet atop blanket stitch stems with French knot centers.

Seed stitch

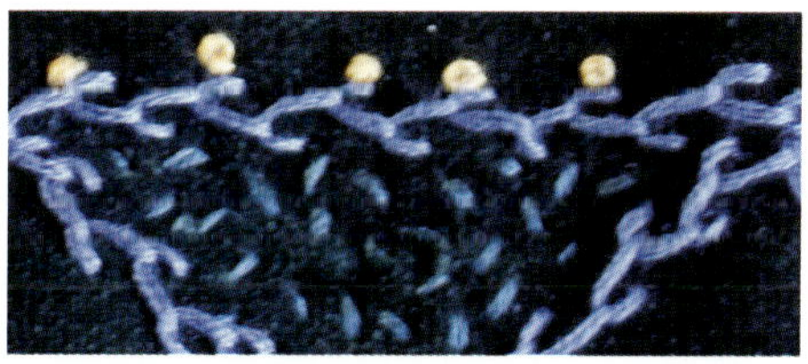

The seed stitch is small, straight stitch. A pattern of seed stitches can be employed to add texture or color to an area. The pattern can be random (as shown in the upper photo with featherstitches and French knots) or more regimented (as shown in the lower photo, tucked between the rows of corduroy wale).

Woolen Wow!

This stocking might appear intimidating initially, with the many small pieces that make up several of the sections.

You can simplify the design considerably by using one piece of red, green, or light purple wool instead of the many smaller pieces in sections 1, 2, 4, and 7.

If you wish to tackle the more complex version, the outlines above show sections that were sewn together first, and then treated as single pieces when sewn onto the base.

Hanging loop options

Folded fabric

Satin ribbon

Crocheted cord

Grosgrain ribbon

SPECIFIC TO **WOOLEN WOW!**

Woolen fabrics:
Navy blue, pink, olive green, red, and purple

Woolen embroidery floss:
Navy blue, olive green, red, pink, and purple

Monochrome Magic

This monochromatic beauty was done in shades of cream, beige, and tan. The juxtaposition of the textures heightens the visual interest.

Texture combinations

Velvet, moiré, velveteen, and rayon in shades from bright to deep purple delight the eye.

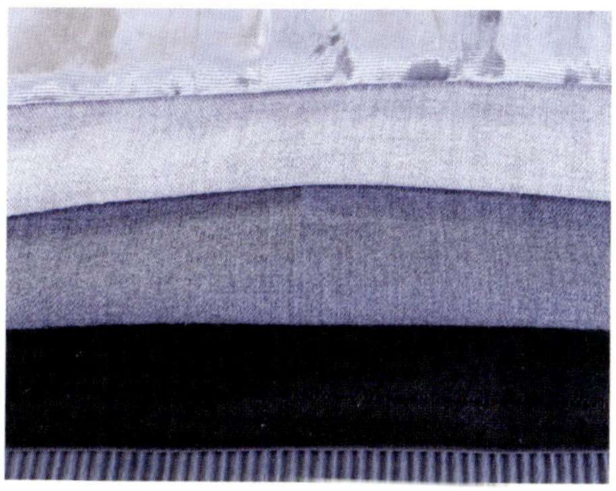

Crushed velvet, silk, linen, wool, velveteen, and corduroy are elegant in shades of gray.

Crushed taffeta, organza, taffeta, moiré, and velvet contrast in soothing greens.

As you plan with textures

Think about the tactile characteristics of different fabrics.

- A loose weave, such as linen, contrasts nicely with a tight weave, such as taffeta.
- A high sheen, such as satin, contrasts nicely with a dull sheen, such as velvet.
- A high pile, such as corduroy, contrasts nicely with the smooth finish of silk.

SPECIFIC TO **MONOCHROME MAGIC**

Fabrics:

Eggshell beige raw silk
Gold organza
Ivory sateen
Natural linen
Desert sand velveteen
Tan corduroy
Ivory raw silk

Embroidery floss:

Ivory, tan, linen, metallic gold, and ivory silk

Rachel's Homecoming

Wreath pattern

You may use the drawing above as a guide for stitching your wreath or as a literal pattern. It shows how one leg of each featherstitch follows the circle shape closely. The berries (trios of French knots) can be placed as regularly or randomly as you wish.

You can stitch your wreath more easily on a thin fabric, such as satin, silk, or linen, than on a thick fabric.

Some crafters use a drinking glass or a lid to draw the wreath base circle. Tailor's chalk in pencil form works nicely to draw your guide and brushes off easily when you are finished.

Embellishment options

Options for embellishment include beading (as above), crocheted lace, and ribbon. You can buy strips of beading at your local craft store.

Embroidered name

You may choose to hand-embroider a name, as on Rachel's stocking. You may also have it machine stitched at a commercial shop as on Anna's stocking, shown above.

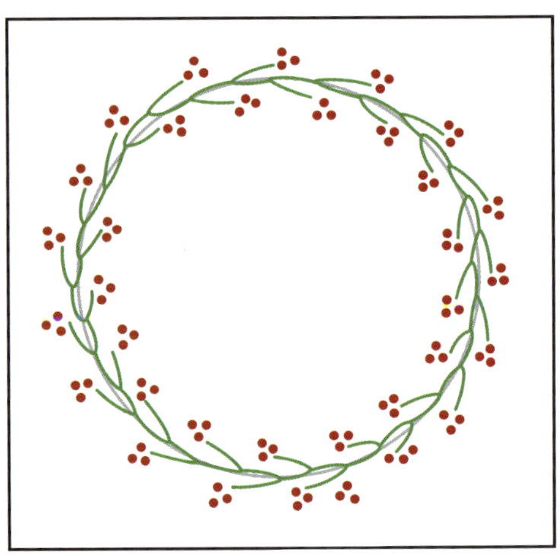

Enlarge pattern 150% for actual size.

SPECIFIC TO **RACHEL'S HOMECOMING**

Fabrics:
- Eggshell beige and ivory raw silk
- Olive green organza
- Forest green velveteen
- Brown and black velvet
- Gold and olive green taffeta
- Rust/black and olive green crushed taffeta

Embroidery floss:
- Rust, forest green, ivory silk, and silver metallic

Beads:
- Ivory and black
- Black beading fringe

Distelfink Delight

Distelfink pattern

The distelfink, a stylized goldfinch, often appears in Pennsylvania German-influenced artwork. It is said to symbolize happiness and good fortune.

Working with wool

The weave of wool makes it very easy for the needle to glide through the fabric while embroidering.

Along with color considerations, you can add visual interest to your all-wool stocking by varying the weight of the wool fabric and the tightness of the weave.

You may consider working with hand-dyed wool. The irregularity of the color saturation, illustrated in the pink, gold, and olive green wool below, lends a delightful air of authenticity to your creation.

Hand-dyed wool

SPECIFIC TO **DISTELFINK DELIGHT**

The color palette here is identical to *Woolen Wow!* on page 14. The new piecing, color arrangement, and embroidery give it a completely different look.

Woolen Fabrics:
Navy blue, pink, olive green, red, and purple

Woolen embroidery floss:
Navy blue, purple, olive green, pink, and red

Remembering Grandma

The riot of color, seemingly casual patch arrangement, and generous use of velvet give this stocking a nostalgic feel. The richness of the embroidery thread enhances the look.

As illustrated on page 14, small pieces are sometimes sewn together into a larger strip or block, and then sewn onto the base as a single patch. Patches 4, 5, 8, and 11 in this stocking were done using that method.

Color ideas

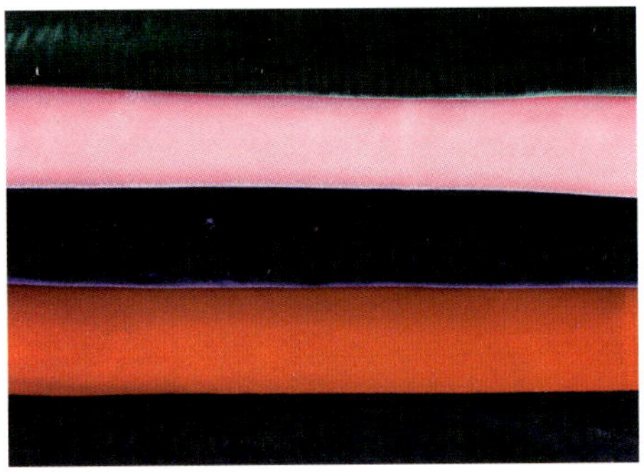

The rich jewel tones of green, pink, purple, and red zing against the black.

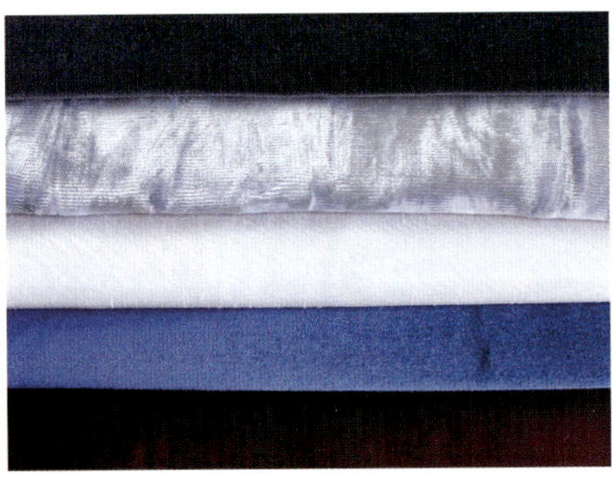

A deep burgundy contrasts with the cooler slate gray, silver, white, and blue.

Update a classic with shades of hot pink against cool grays.

You can't go wrong with traditional reds and greens, from subdued to bright.

SPECIFIC TO **REMEMBERING GRANDMA**

Fabrics:

- Maroon and gold taffeta
- Brown and green moiré
- Blue raw silk
- Gold and dark green velveteen
- Dark blue, light blue, and reddish-brown velvet
- Blue satin

Embroidery floss:

Gold, blue, teal, light brown, green, dark brown, dark green, and metallic gold

AMAZING SPACE

SPACE TELESCOPES

BY LORI DITTMER

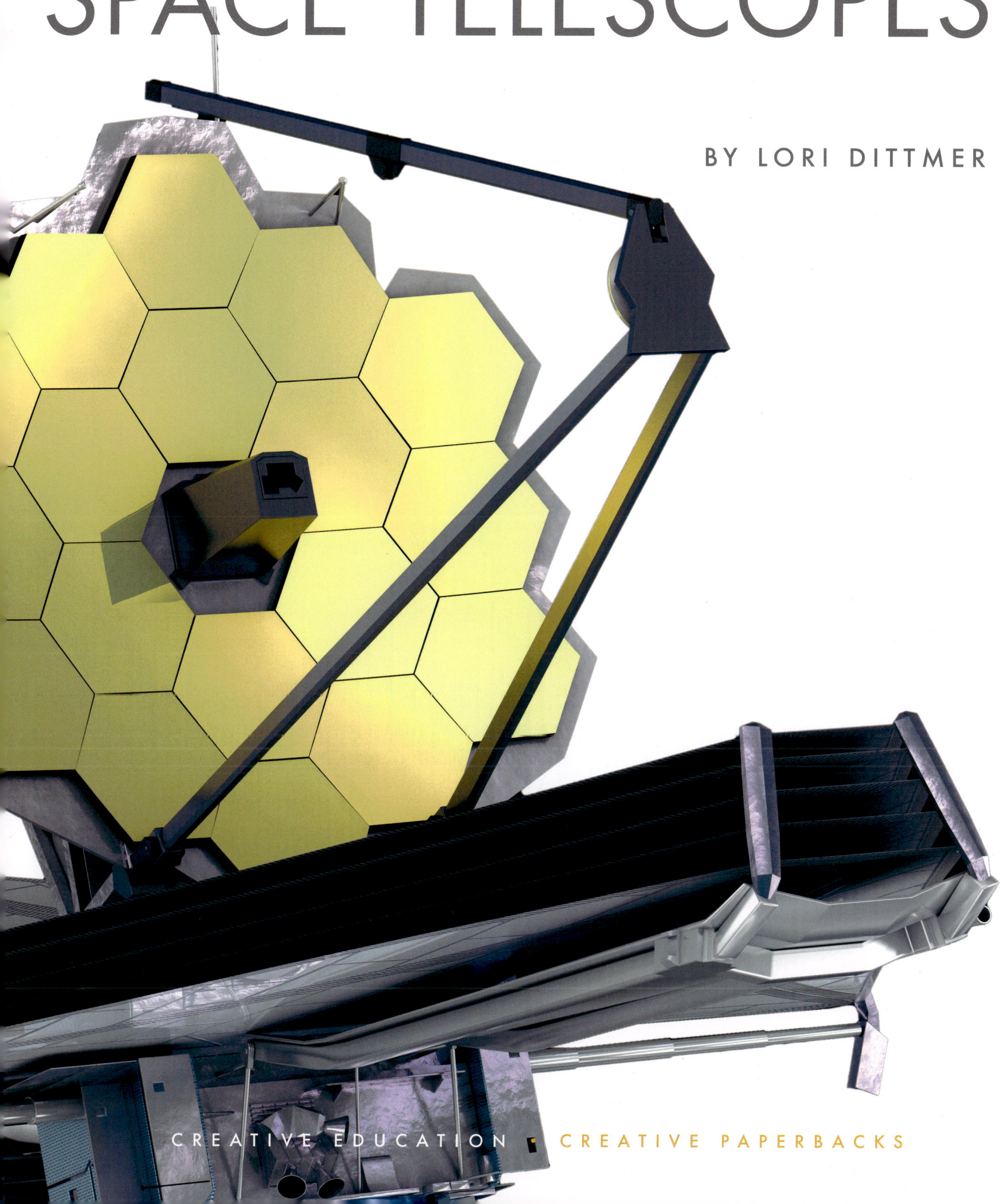

CREATIVE EDUCATION • CREATIVE PAPERBACKS

Published by Creative Education
and Creative Paperbacks
P.O. Box 227, Mankato, Minnesota 56002
Creative Education and Creative Paperbacks
are imprints of The Creative Company
www.thecreativecompany.us

Design by The Design Lab
Art direction by Graham Morgan
Edited by Ana Brauer

Photographs: Alamy Stock Photo/Alexandr Mitiuc, cover, 1, 22; NASA/Unknown, 9, 18, 21, Chris Gunn, 5, ESA, 7, ESA, and M. Livio and the Hubble 20th Anniversary Team (STScI), 8, Goddard, 6, Goddard/Chris Gunn, 2, 17, Goddard/SDO, 13; Wikimedia Commons/NASA, 10, 14, 16, 20

Library of Congress Cataloging-in-Publication Data
Names: Dittmer, Lori, author.
Title: Space telescopes / by Lori Dittmer.
Other titles: Amazing space (Creative Education, Inc. (Mankato, Minn.))
Description: Mankato, Minnesota : Creative Education and Creative Paperbacks, [2025] | Series: Amazing space | Includes bibliographical references and index. | Audience: Ages 6–9 | Audience: Grades 2–3 | Summary: "Learn about space telescopes and how the tools help with research and discovery. This astronomy title for elementary-aged kids includes captions, on-page definitions, a space science feature, additional STEM resources, and an index"—Provided by publisher.
Identifiers: LCCN 2024018575 (print) | LCCN 2024018576 (ebook) | ISBN 9798889892342 (library binding) | ISBN 9781682776001 (paperback) | ISBN 9798889893455 (ebook) Subjects: LCSH: Space telescopes—Juvenile literature. | Orbiting astronomical observatories—Juvenile literature. Classification: LCC QB500.267 .D58 2025 (print) |LCC QB500.267 (ebook) |DDC 522/.2919—dc23/eng/20240509
LC record available at https://lccn.loc.gov/2024018575
LC ebook record available at https://lccn.loc.gov/2024018576

Printed in China